tantrums

last straw strategies

D0064247

last straw strategies

99 tips to bring you back from the end of your rope

tantrums

Michelle Kennedy

BARRON'S

First edition for the United States, its territories
and possessions, and Canada published in 2003 by
BARRON'S EDUCATIONAL SERIES, INC.
by arrangement with
THE IVY PRESS LIMITED

All inquiries should be addressed to:
Barron's Educational Series, Inc.,
250 Wireless Boulevard
Hauppauge, New York 11788
www.barronseduc.com

Every effort has been taken to ensure that all
information in this book is correct. This book is not
intended to replace consultation with your doctor,
surgeon, or other healthcare professional. The author
and publisher disclaim any loss, injury, or damage
incurred as a consequence, directly or indirectly, of
the use and application of the contents of this book.

International Standard Book Number
0-7641-2441-2

Library of Congress Catalog Card No.
2002108551

This book was conceived,
designed, and produced by
THE IVY PRESS LIMITED
The Old Candlemakers
West Street
Lewes
East Sussex BN7 2NZ

Creative Director PETER BRIDGEWATER
Publisher SOPHIE COLLINS
Editorial Director STEVE LUCK
Design Manager TONY SEDDON
Project Editor MANDY GREENFIELD
Designer JANE LANAWAY
Illustrator EMMA BROWNJOHN

Printed in China by
Hong Kong Graphics & Printing Ltd.
9 8 7 6 5 4 3 2 1

contents

tantrums
introduction

It's a beautiful day in the neighborhood, and with one of my cherubic children, I am dawdling through the market. I am at my most patient, pointing out interesting things, explaining the difference between a pineapple and a regular apple . . . generally at my parenting best. Then, like a storm that appears out of nowhere, it hits. Lightly at first. The question, "Can I have that?" is the beginning of the storm, the wind picking up. "And that?" is the rustling in the trees. But I haven't brought my umbrella, because this is a perfect day, and I refuse to let anything ruin it. So, cheerfully and in my most singsongy voice, I reply, "No." But it no longer matters; my cheeriness won't help. The storm rears its ugly head. "Waaahhhh!!$#@$^& . . . " and on it goes. The screaming and crying may be accompanied by any amount of kicking, biting, throwing, banging fists, or laying on the floor. Over the years my children have laid out a veritable smorgasbord of tantrums, from the traditional to the unusual.

No other behavior can be as infuriating, embarrassing, and sometimes downright comical as the temper tantrum. Hopefully, the tips in the following nine sections will help you survive them, avoid them, and maintain your sense of humor, because when we're faced with a screaming, red-faced child, humor is just about the only thing we parents have left.

you're in charge

There is nothing worse than dragging a screaming child through a grocery store. Nothing. And the number of people who will look at you disdainfully, clucking their tongues, will equal the number of people who will come up to you and tell you what their parents did to them when they were little. So, if you can, try and have the patience to listen to the "In my day . . ." stories as you craftily drag your limp noodle child through the aisle to the door. Also don't forget—the parents are in charge. If I remember anything about all those parenting books I had time to read when I was pregnant, it was that they told me I was in charge. Repeat it to yourself as a mantra while dragging said child (now kicking and biting your arm) out to the car. "I'm in charge, I'm in charge."

feel the force

2-4 years

Believe your child is capable of behaving, and that she *will* listen to you. For years I got this advice and it didn't seem to be enough, but as I gained more confidence I realized how true it is. Ever notice how some mothers can stop unwanted behavior with just a glance? Once you are consistent enough to enforce your rules every time, not ever "giving in" when it seems easier, then your child will live up to your expectations. This may sound easier said than done, but don't dismiss it until you have tried it. And stick to it.

9

tough love

You are not their friend. I know you want to be. It's hard to think of ourselves as the "mean Mommy," but get over it, quick. There is nothing more annoying than witnessing a previously intelligent adult actually trying to reason a three-year-old out of a can of soda in the grocery store.

"But it's not good for you," says mom, pleadingly. "I want drink," Cory the Defiant says. "But we can't today, I don't have enough money," mother tries again. "I want drink! I want drink!" You can tell where this is going. Solution? Take can of drink from screaming child, place back on

shelf, then place screaming child under arm and march out of store. Customers throughout will applaud both your superior parenting skills and your leaving! There are times when reasoning with your child may be appropriate, but this is not one of them.

you're in charge
explain the mission

This works great for me. I assemble all four of my children outside the grocery store. "We are only buying milk, eggs, bread, and chicken," I say to them sternly. "We are not buying cookies, candy, toys, or anything else. Anyone who asks for anything is grounded. Period. Got it?" They nod in agreement. And after they ask and I follow through with a grounding, they don't do it again.

mean what you say 2-4 years

Don't threaten it, if you don't really mean it. I have a crystal-clear image in my head of my father when I was a child. And his voice saying, "If I get up out of this chair . . . " is just as clear. He only needed to say that, and start to get up out of the chair, for us rowdy kids either to be quiet or immediately scatter off to another part of the house. He never did get up out of that chair, and I doubt that much would have happened if he did. But the threat was good enough. We didn't want to find out what would happen next. Make good on your threats, too. Don't be afraid to "turn this car around," or "leave everything in the shopping cart and go home."

you're in charge
2-4 years
try not to lose it . . .

It is so easy. Sometimes you might just want to yell at everything in sight. Before you sentence your child to a lifetime of scrubbing the tub with a toothbrush, make her sit somewhere and not move while you take a walk around the yard for a minute. Take the time to devise a really creative punishment, if the child is older, or just think happy thoughts. Come back to her able to speak in calm, level tones.

... but if you do

2-4 years

We all do—it's inevitable. One day you're going to blow
up. You're going to scream, or maybe even spank (it's not
right, but it happens) your child. And when it does happen,
your child is going to look up at you with those little puppy
dog eyes wondering where on earth he got such an awful
parent—or he might be too shocked to wonder anything at
all! Step back. Take a deep breath (or three). Apologize for the
way you yelled at (or spanked) him. Tell him what you did
was wrong, but at the same time explain why you were so
angry. Don't say, "Well, if you hadn't hit your sister, I wouldn't
have hit you." That's just putting the blame on your child.
Approach it from a "we both have to concentrate on calming
down when something makes us angry" point of view. Your
child needs to know that just because your behavior wasn't
right, it doesn't mean you condone what he did.

let's hear it for
the good stuff

Don't just let your children know when they are doing
something wrong. Let them know when they are doing
something right, too. Make your expectations clear and then
when they are met, praise your children, particularly if they
do something without being asked. "Thank you so much for
picking up that toy when you were done with that. I really
appreciate it." My kids always loved to hear me say that

I was impressed with something they did—or tried to do. "Are you pressed, Mama?" I would often hear. If you make a real effort to be "pressed" by the good stuff, then your children won't have a reason to try and get your attention with bad behavior.

2-4 years **suitable treatment**

Use discipline that makes sense, especially if your child is very young and may not have known that what he did was wrong. Say your toddler tears up a book. It could have just been a load of fun to him. Pick up the pieces and, if you can, let him help you tape the book back together, telling him, "Books are much more fun when all of the pages are together."

judge the action

2-4 years

Try to avoid saying harmful things like, "That was stupid,"
or worse. Making your child understand that you didn't like
what he did, but that you still like him, is essential. It's also
important to watch how you say things, or suddenly you'll
have a child who doubts his every move. "I don't like it when
you ignore me" is much better than something like, "You're
so stupid, you never listen!" It's easy to say something
harmful just to make a point. A better way to make that
point is to let your child know how he makes you feel when
he talks to you in that way or ignores you, or whatever.

don't buy into guilt

Let your child know that you really don't care if his friend has the latest Nintendo system. I have often told my foursome that it is not my job to buy them every new toy that comes down the pike. It is my job to keep them healthy, clean, fed, and get them educated before I send them on their way—everything else is voluntary! If you feel good about bringing home a treat —then go for it. But if your kids beg, plead, and won't be quiet until you say yes —that's spoiling.

be consistent

Nothing will work if your partner, child care provider, or even you yourself lets your child off a punishment imposed by another caregiver. Let the parent (or the caregiver) who discovered the bad behavior carry out the punishment—and don't dispute the punishment in front of the child (unless, of course, it's something really bad or abusive). Disputing the punishment in front of the child will only teach him to play you off each other. If you really have a problem with the way a punishment was handled, discuss it away from the child, determine how to correct the situation, and then let the person who originally punished the child fix it. This way no one seems to come in to "save the day," and the child still knows that the person who imposed the punishment is to be respected.

instant
calmer

They come up like a storm. First it's the rubbing of the eyes, signifying the growing wind. Then it's just one too many requests for bubble gum or a new toy after you've already said, "No" three or four times. And then it hits . . . The tantrum. The storm of the toddler we all dread. They are natural, sure, but there are also ways to prevent them and to deal with them when they are happening.

do I have your attention?

2–4 years

Toddlers do not always respond to commands from on high—often they just hear NSS (non-specific shouting) when they're too busy concentrating on shouting themselves. Get on your knees in front of your child, hold him gently but firmly by the shoulders, and look at him until you have established eye contact. Then speak. That way your message is likely to cross the great divide.

instant calmer
ignore it (the behavior,
not your kid)

During the toddler years there are lots of things they will simply outgrow. For example, right now my son loves to rearrange the pantry. I figure in a few short months this will be just a memory, so why expect him to learn not to do it? It's pointless to waste time and energy, and it's frustrating if, in a little while, he moves on and the problem ceases to exist. Okay, it might be replaced with another, but the next problem might be easier to solve.

respect the tantrum

2-4 years

Acknowledge your child's feelings, but don't let them rule your actions. When my little guy is in the midst of a full-blown hissy fit, I simply look at him and say, "Wow! You're really mad. Let me know when you're done." And then—and this is key—I walk away (obviously making sure there is nothing he can hurt himself on nearby). This way he knows that I do care about his feelings, but that I'm not going to listen to him rave and that it's certainly not the best way for him to get what he wants. And he has the opportunity to come tell me why he's mad after he's calmed down.

instant calmer
another place

Sometimes a child will frighten herself with the strength
of her outburst and find that she doesn't know how to put
an end to it. Pick her up and hold her close to you (so she
cannot flail her arms and legs) and get out of the room,
or store, and away from other people, to give her space to
calm down. When you are away from the tantrum arena,
keep her in a big hug (kneel down if necessary) and count
slowly to 100 out loud. This will help you as well. If it isn't
possible to take your child out of the situation, try the

birdcage maneuver. Pick up the child, hold her close, and cover (loosely!) her face with a scarf or her blanket for a few seconds. This is a bit like throwing a cloth over the cage of a squawking parrot. As far as the child is concerned, she is in another place, where she can calm down and regroup.

dancing out of trouble

2–4 years

Sometimes tantrums are a great way (or at least the child thinks so) to blow off steam. If your child has got herself into a tantrum loop—which usually means she has forgotten the trigger for the whole thing—put on your favorite dance music and show her your best moves. Your actions will be so unexpected that she'll probably stop howling and sometimes even join in. If dancing is not your thing, try some running around the house.

take a
breather

2-4 years

The opposite could also be true. Your child could be getting frustrated because he's tired or maybe trying too hard at the activity at hand. Is he trying to button his coat for the fifth time and it's just not happening? If so, take a seat with him, bring out a book, and rest for a bit. It's almost guaranteed that, with a clear head and a fresh start, buttoning that coat will be much easier the second time around.

instant calmer
the quarterback response

I just love it when my child gets angry and then throws whatever he's playing with across the room! No, of course not, and whether or not he has Brett Favre's arm, a child needs to know that throwing things is not an acceptable way to be angry. When my child is angry enough to throw something, I hold him firmly by the shoulders and tell him to take some deep breaths. Sometimes he cries and says, "I can't." So, I breathe with him. The aim is to eventually get him to take a few breaths next time before he throws something.

get in
on the act

2-4 years

Get down on the floor and yell and scream just as loudly and just as vigorously as your child. This behavior will probably shock her and then, after the initial reaction, she will almost certainly start to laugh, although it might take longer for some children to crack a smile than others. Just the sight of a supposedly grown-up person having a full-blown fit does the trick. This method works because if you can both laugh about a tantrum, you can become pals again, too. And it's a great tactic with really small children because most of their tantrums aren't about anything specific.

instant calmer

1-3 years
food fight

A toddler can get bored in her high chair and start to throw food. This isn't uncommon, but it is annoying and messy (Okay, more than messy!). There are a few things you can do to prevent this. First, try to teach your child the word "down." When she looks as though she's done, say, "Do you want to get down?" Serve realistic portions. You can always give her more, but if the amount in front of her seems insurmountable, some of it is going to land on the floor. Be aware of how close your child is to finishing: put her down as soon as she's done.

avoid the problem

When my older children head for school for the day, my toddler who remains at home suddenly believes that none of the normal rules apply to him . . . and he heads for the fridge. All of a sudden, at some horrible hour like 8 A.M. he's asking for cookies and Tootsie Rolls I didn't even know I had. And it goes on all day. If your child is demanding— let's say, a snack—what seems to be 50 times a day, then try changing his mealtime schedules to half an hour earlier, or let him have healthy snacks many times a day. When the options before lunch are restricted to carrots and celery, you might find your wee one is not quite as hungry as he thought he was.

take them outside

2-4 years

If you have both been cooped up together in the house for the day, your toddler (and you) may be a little stir-crazy. The weather may be terrible, but fresh air and a break from your own four walls will be just what you both need. Wrap her up warm, stick the child in the stroller, and go for a walk around the block or in a nearby park.

When my own kids were small, the effort of taking them out sometimes seemed too much. (Remember, you are sometimes just as strung-out as your child!) When this happened, I used to take a big blanket or throw, fold up my little one in it, and then simply walk around our tiny yard. The outdoor magic worked even in such a limited space.

spankless
options

 I am not a spanking parent. I believe that one of
the worst things you can do to children is hit them to
illustrate your power over them. One of my own mistakes
demonstrated to me how senseless hitting can be. I was
playing on the floor with my first-born (then almost two)
and a neighbor's child about the same age, whom I was
baby-sitting. My darling boy, in order to prove whatever
point his wee brain was trying to make, hit our guest in
the face. My intelligent response? To slap his hand to
show him that hitting was wrong. No, really, I did. But
I looked at him, tears streaming down his shocked face,
and couldn't believe that I thought what I had done
actually made sense. Where was my brain? Who knows?
I think it came out with the baby.

corner stop

2-4 years

My three-year-old daughter is very headstrong and has a tendency to do whatever she wants, regardless of the consequences. So I started sending her to the corner of a room for 10 to 20 seconds when she misbehaved.

It doesn't seem like much time, but it's long enough for her to calm down and regain control of herself, yet not so long that she gets up and walks away out of sheer boredom from standing in a corner. It's working well so far.

spankless options
2-4 years
on the bench

A time-out can be effective, but it doesn't necessarily have to be long. One minute per year of age is sometimes all that is necessary, especially for a young child, to get himself together and calm down. Pick a certain place, a boring place, where your child can sit, uninterrupted. On the other hand, on occasion I have found that making the child sit out and watch while everyone else is still playing is also a good incentive for better behavior. It all depends on you and the child (and the offending behavior). If a child refuses to stay in time-out or remains hysterical, I have sat in the time-out with him in my lap, rocking him and talking softly to him.

sleeping it off
2-4 years

First, don't let a nap or going to bed be the actual
punishment. Have an intermediate location, like the
sofa or a chair, as a "time-out" place, where a screaming
child can calm down. Then, if it's very obvious your child is
sleepy (and now calmer), take her to bed. Using the bed as
a punishment place will only cause bedtime problems later
on, when she associates her bedroom with the chastisement
that was meted out earlier in the day.

spankless options

2-4 years

chill time

Use a timer. This can be good for both you and your child. Set a timer for five or ten minutes and inform your child that he may not get up out of his time-out spot for the duration. This also gives you five or ten minutes to be by yourself (keeping an ear out for a wandering child, of course). Use the timer in concert with a "quiet place." In this way, the two will be connected in your child's mind. And if your child is very young, set the timer for only a minute or two—this doesn't give you much of a break, but it does reinforce the idea that a time-out has a time limit.

toy time-out

Does the offending behavior have something to do with a toy? Designate a shelf in the closet where disputed toys can have their own time-out. This is particularly useful if a favorite stuffed animal suddenly becomes a weapon-wielding bad guy.

spankless options

2-4 years   **no option**

Don't set yourself up for a fall. One of the worst things a
mom can do is ask her two-year-old's opinion as to whether
he should have lunch or keep playing. Also, don't ask your
child for permission to do something. Asking, "Can I put Mr.
Bunny here while we eat lunch?" is only setting yourself up

for a tantrum. Just say in a matter-of-fact voice: "Mr. Bunny is going to sit on the couch while we eat our lunch," and then take your child's hand and lead him away. You'd be surprised at how much trouble you can avoid when you don't ask your little one's opinion!

tell it just like it is

2-4 years

Be specific. Just saying, "Be good," on the way to Grandma's is not enough. You have to be specific. Tell your child about using "inside" and "outside" voices. Let her know she'll have to sit still at dinner, but will be able to run around outside afterward. Tell her to say thank you if Grandma gives her a present.

accentuate the positive

2-4 years

Show your child that you care, by saying, "I love you," and "You're really important and special to me." Make sure that you find time to praise his talents. Don't use sarcasm or kidding in order to point out his weaknesses. Instead, try to be positive and encouraging about his strong points. Reward good behavior, and have *fun* together—these positive parenting strategies are the most effective ones in teaching children to be well behaved! Never ignore good behavior, because then there is simply no incentive for your child to repeat it on another occasion.

2-4 years   **take a break**

My daughter is a very active child who
requires a lot of attention and control.
Sometimes it is inevitable
that I'll get mad! When
she cut her hair for the
fourth time, I was livid.
All parents get angry,
and that's why I am a

real believer in time-out. And by that I mean not just for kids, but for mom as well. When my daughter's in time-out, I go to another room to gather myself and get ready to discipline her in a rational manner. It's a time for me to organize my thoughts and get past the fury, without taking that anger out on her. You're not a bad mommy just because you get angry! Nobody can remain calm and collected all the time, so have some time to yourself.

2-4 years

a middle way

Use reasonable consequences. This one works particularly well if the child isn't in a full-blown tantrum, but is stomping and yelling around the house. "If you must do that," I say, "go and do it in your room." He'll go, possibly slamming the door behind him, but he'll probably be back in a minute or two, because being angry in a room by yourself isn't nearly as effective as showing off in front of your parents!

spankless options

set some targets 2-4 years

Tell yourself that you aren't going to lose it or yell before lunchtime. This will force you to find different ways to deal with your anger and frustration. When something really sets you off, just think to yourself, "I'm not going to yell (or spank) . . . " and then talk in a sweet voice—even syrupy if you have to—to your child. You'll be amazed at the creative ways you'll find to deal with your child when you eliminate the shout from your repertoire.

A good yell sure has a place, but it loses force if you overuse it. Use a strong yell wisely—this way your kids will know that you mean business when you do.

when your kid's
the bully

Young children don't always have the verbal ability or the mental/emotional restraint required to express anger or frustration without lashing out. It can be shocking to a mom and dad when the kid in the sandbox doing the biting or hitting turns out to be their own. As long as you act swiftly and correct the situation (using the tips on the following pages), then you should be able to avoid any major embarrassments.

when your Kid's the bully
give them space

2-4 years

Don't hover. It is so easy as parents to try and control our children's play. But sometimes children play "to" us—acting out for the attention it brings. Leave children alone (or as alone as you can) and usually they will solve their disputes on their own, without resorting to help from you.

2-4 years
change of scene

If your child is often aggressive with other children, maybe he doesn't get to spend enough time with other kids his age. My youngest, for example, is very used to playing with his older siblings, but has little experience with children his own age. Enrolling your child in preschool, even for just two half days a week, or organizing a play group with other moms and dads, can do wonders for improving your child's social skills.

take them away

2-4 years

If your child is really getting out of hand, and possibly
even hurting other children, remove her from the scene.
There is no need to make the other kids suffer because of
her tantrum! Have her sit by herself for a moment or two,
and let her know that the same rules you use at home are in
effect with other children, too.

share options

Make a "for other children" toy box. Often, small children are very protective of their favorite toys and it hurts them to watch other children playing with them. Give your child the opportunity to divide some of his toys into those that are acceptable for other children to play with and those that are not. Take the real favorites to a closet and let your child know that his favorite stuffed animal or truck will be "out of the mix" for the day. But also make it clear that this means that the other children get to play with the rest and that this has to be okay.

when your kid's the bully
the same rulebook

2-4 years

It's bad enough when the parents of the same child disagree on discipline, but when you get several moms together, the variety is endless. Agree on some ground rules. If it really offends you to have someone else discipline your child, let the other parents know that, if there is a problem, they should let you know first, then you'll take care of it. I have a particular friend with whom I am so comfortable that we yell at each other's children interchangeably and no one's feelings are ever hurt—in fact, we usually cheer each other on! But that isn't always the case, and you need to respect not only other children's feelings, but also other parents' feelings.

playdate
rehearsal

2-4 years

Do a little role playing with
your child before friends
come over or before you
go to see friends. Sit
down on the floor
with him and play
with something.
Make your child ask
you if he can play with
it. Then say no. Let your child know that it's all right to ask
if there is another toy to play with. Think up a couple of
different scenarios like this that your child might face, and
practice making the right responses.

don't go
over the top

2-4 years

When your child is aggressive, try not to overreact. It's likely that you'll scare the living daylights out of both your child and the one she's harassing. And don't lecture your child in the middle of a playdate. Not because it's embarrassing to the child, but because you're paying more attention to the topic than is probably necessary. Besides, she won't understand half of what you say anyway. It will sound more like, "Blah, blah, blah, no . . . blah, blah, blah, bite . . . " The best way to deal with this situation is either to swiftly remove the child or firmly say a few choice words, making it clear you will not tolerate poor behavior.

2-4 years **biting**

It was one thing when my baby bit me when he was nursing; it was another thing when as a toddler he bit me on the shoulder! Fortunately (at least for other children), I was his main target and the reason was usually tiredness, but still! If your child is biting other children (or you), immediately take him away and let him know in no uncertain terms that biting is not acceptable. Even a two-year-old understands "No," so just say in a clear tone, "No biting" and have him take a seat. It's quick, concise, clear, and effective. Will it keep him from biting ever again? Maybe not, but if he knows there are consequences to his action—eventually he'll stop.

something to bite on   2-4 years

For some children, I have been told, biting is more an oral fixation than an actual desire to cause pain. If this appears to be the case with your child, give her a washcloth or a hard, rubber teething ring specifically for this purpose, so that she has something specific to bite on. Alternatively, if your child is not biting out of aggression (more of a teething or gnawing kind of bite), give her something edible to chew on while she plays, like a bagel. She could be in a bit of toddler pain from incoming molars and doesn't understand what is causing her desire to bite.

March your child right up to the offended child and make him say he's sorry. Have him give back the toy he took or offer a cookie as a peace offering, and if the other parent and child are amenable, maybe have him give him a hug.

when your kid's the bully
punching bags

Sometimes my oldest two, who are just 14 months apart in age, would really get angry with each other. If they were getting into it over something, usually a 25-cent toy from a yard sale missing an eye (definitely something I could never figure out why they were even playing with it, much less fighting over it), I would separate them—telling them they were "not allowed" to play with each other—and would give them each a pillow to toss around or pound on. They usually got their aggression out quickly and would soon be begging me to let them play together again.

at home with
mr. or ms. manners

Bill Cosby once said that children are selfish, greedy, and will do anything to get what they want. That may be so, but if it is, I at least want my kids to be polite about it. "Please" and "thank you" aren't just words, and they aren't where politeness ends. Politeness is also saying thank you for a gift, even though you already have an identical one, or knowing not to point out, at the family reunion, that Aunt Anna has a huge wart on her nose.

cut the phone chat

Are the kids always tugging on your clothes when you're on the phone, demanding attention? That might mean you're on the phone too much. By limiting your conversations to ten minutes or so, you will be able to train your children

to be patient for the time it takes to have a reasonable phone conversation. Make important (or just fun) calls when your children are napping or after they go to bed at night.

2-4 years **build an extension**

Get an old phone that doesn't work and put it near your phone—then your child can talk while you're talking. Alternatively, put his toy phone on a lower table, but still near the phone. Then you can both answer when it rings.

use a timer

It's late. You're making dinner, trying to feed the dog, and trying to talk to the president of the school fundraiser about the fun-filled week she has in store for you—all at the same time. And then . . . the whining voice that says, "Do we have to eat that for dinner?" Or something equally annoying. If your child is constantly after your undivided attention and you have something urgent to finish, use a timer. Don't set it for too long (ten minutes is a long time to a child). Tell her you will give her your attention when the bell rings. To develop trust, when the timer does ring, stop what you're doing and give her some time.

good signs

Not all communication has to be verbal. One mom describes a board she has at home that has "Hi," "I'm bored," and "Emergency" written on it. If she is on the phone when the children come home, they can check one off. If they check "I'm bored," she reaches into a drawer and picks out

a slip of paper that has a chore or project listed on it. If they check "Emergency," there had better really be one! You could also add "I'm hungry" and "I'm thirsty" to the list. This tip works better with older children, but you could always use pictures instead of words for the young ones.

visitors

2-4 years

If someone comes over, even if it's just the cable guy to sort out your house's wiring, and you need to speak with him, make introductions. Introduce your child to the person, tell her that this is so-and-so and that he came over to fix the lighting, or whatever. Then say, "I'll have to speak to him quite a bit, so go and play and I'll let you know when it's time to say good-bye."

excuse me

It's a miracle that when I go to sleep every night, I don't have the sound of voices clammering in my head. Well, sometimes I do, but it's usually because my children are so excited to tell me how they coaxed the cricket they found outside into their bedroom, or some other such miracle, that they talk over each other, over me, over my husband, and over anyone else who dares try to talk to us. Frankly, I got a wee bit tired of the constant interrupting, so my children and I had a little class that I called "Interrupting 101: Why Mom hates it." Teach your children the words "excuse me," and show them how to use them. Be warned; my children took it to mean that if they said it, they could just start talking! So, make sure you practice proper "excuse me" etiquette—otherwise you'll get "excuse me, excuse me, *excuse me*!"

joining in

Do you really need to exclude them? Let them participate.
Instead of constantly sending your child away when you
have a friend over, pour her a glass of milk and let her join
in the conversation. For a time she'll feel like a real grown-
up, but after a while she'll get bored and will want to go off
and play, even on her own.

Sometimes a child throws a tantrum in a new situation because he is forced to be polite to a neighbor or relative he doesn't know. You can avoid this by letting your child know that it's okay not to hug or kiss Aunt Susie and that, if he doesn't want to be touched, he doesn't have to be. Just make sure that you let Aunt Susie know what the ground rules are, too.

accepting gifts

Before a family gathering or party at which your child is to be given presents, take her aside and let her know that, even if she gets a toy she already has, or if she gets something that she doesn't like, she should say thank you and smile and not comment on the gift. Your child might point out that if she says she likes the gift when she doesn't, it is lying, but let her know that smiling and thanking a person for the effort of a present is the polite thing to do. Most kids will want to avoid hurting someone else's feelings.

at home with mr. manners

empathy

A great way to teach your child about rudeness is to be rude. I was tired of the way my children were speaking to each other—so my husband and I put on a little show when I said some not very nice things and he looked hurt. My children immediately jumped to his defense. Of course, I was then able to tell them that that is how they sound when they make fun of each other. A constant reminder in our household is to "treat your sister [or brother] as you would like to be treated." It doesn't stop every rude comment, but it stops quite a few.

big kid

3 years and up

Sometimes older kids regress to tantrums to get more attention than a younger sibling. In this case, try to point out the benefits of being a big kid. Give her responsibilities: not just chores, but big-kid jobs, like paying in the store or making breakfast for herself. You can also look through old pictures or home movies and show that you remember her babyhood as well. But emphasize how proud you are at all that she's accomplished since then, and that you're looking forward to her teaching her sibling all those skills.

gimme, gimme, gimme
and other issues

The "Gimmes" are the bane of every parent's life and the joy of every marketing executive. Is it possible to get through a store checkout line without being asked for one of the treats shelved at just the right height for your little ones? No, definitely not. But it is possible to say no and to mean it. The following tips will help you get out of the store without an additional $100 worth of stuff that you don't need and that your dentist would scold you for.

gimme, gimme, gimme
offer a treat

Bring some fruit, a tempting snack, or a toy in your purse, or let the child buy a treat as you enter the store. If he already has something to look forward to, he may not beg for other things as you go around the store.

gimme, gimme, gimme

stick to the plan

Tell your child ahead of time where you will be going and what you will be buying. For example, say, "We have to go to the mall to get a card for Daddy's present. You can look at the little animal figurines in the store, but we're only going to buy a card." If your child knows what to expect, she will be less likely to try to change your mind. I often hold a little pre-shopping conference outside the front of the store before we go in. I also have a hands-in-pockets rule when we go into small shops with breakables, and have received many "thank yous" from shopkeepers for this. If you have a smart-aleck child, as I do, who says, "But I don't have pockets," get that child to clasp her hands behind her back.

gimme, gimme, gimme
just the one

If you decide to let your child buy something, make it clear that he may have one item. If he asks for more, hold up the first item and the other item he would like. Then ask him which one he wants. Repeat this as many times as necessary, but make sure that you only offer him

two items to choose from. Otherwise he may find it impossible to decide and may become agitated about having to choose between several options.

gimme, gimme, gimme

3 years and up

threaten to leave

And then really do it. Even if you've been shopping for two hours and you have a full cart. Even if you're already in line at the checkout. If your child asks you for one more thing after you have told him 20 times "No," don't give in. Tell him that if he keeps asking, or throws a tantrum over it, you're leaving. Warn your child that all the cookies that are in the cart, all of the cool stuff you were talked into buying, will all go away. And then just leave. It will only happen once—when he knows you mean business, he's more likely to behave next time.

gimme, gimme, gimme
crude, but effective

Bribe 'em. Plain and simple. "If you don't ask me for stuff in the store and you don't whine, I'll take you out for ice cream or we'll stop at the park on the way home." It's not a solution for every problem, but it's worth a try. If they don't behave, definitely don't buy them that ice cream.

gimme, gimme, gimme
mother's helper

Let your child help you make the shopping list. You don't
have to write it—you can always draw pictures. This way
she gets to participate in what's being put on the list, and
she knows ahead of time that you are only going to buy
those things that are actually on it.

gimme, gimme, gimme
cart rage

Does your child hate riding in the cart at the supermarket? (I don't know how they could possibly hate being pushed around a busy store—I wish someone would push me sometimes!) My child does, but sometimes in a busy store, you just can't make exceptions. So don't. Make the rules quite clear to them. "Ride in the cart, or you have to hold on to the cart." Undoubtedly they'll pick walking, but also make it clear to them that if they try and run off—then they go right back into the cart. No exceptions to the rule. And then . . . follow through on your threat!

gimme, gimme, gimme

learning about money

My four-year-old loves to pay. So often I will give him just a dollar and let him pick out a small treat. Before I load my items up, he can go to the counter and buy his own item. He feels important, and he also knows that he can only get the one thing. Besides, he spends so much time looking for his item that it usually takes his mind off the shopping I'm doing. And you can tell him, when he picks up an item that's too expensive, that he only has one dollar to spend and that it costs too much, so he must look for something else! That's a good lesson to learn.

gimme, gimme, gimme
having fun in line

Read to your children while you are waiting in line. Bring along a book and read a story while you're standing there. Why not? It will keep the kids' minds off the impulse items and make the waiting a whole lot easier.

gimme, gimme, gimme
2-4 years
bookworm

I heard a great tip years ago from child psychologist and author Penelope Leach, which worked well for me. She said that over the years her children had learned that she always said no when they asked for toys, but if they asked for a book, they were almost guaranteed to get it. My own kids now know the same thing—as a result, they have more books than most kids of their age and they have read them all! Other choices might work for other moms. Just make it really clear what is acceptable to you and what isn't— and then stick to those rules.

gimme, gimme, gimme
let them shop

2-4 years

Instead of making your children follow you passively through the store, let them help pick out items. Tell them you need three boxes of pasta and then let them find the neatest shapes and put them in the cart. If they can read, let them help you find the cheapest item. If you keep them busy picking out your food, and talking about the dinners you'll make with it, they shouldn't have time to ask for anything else!

some cheese
with your whine?

With whining, sometimes it's not even the question,
it's the tone. How I hate to hear it . . . It's worse than
fingernails on a blackboard or fire alarms. And if you let
the whiner win, the whining will never stop. The key
to winning over whining is to not reward them at all for
the tone. Even if they're asking you if they can wash your
car—don't let them if they've asked in a whining tone!

Some cheese with your whine?
I've gone deaf

"I can't hear you."
Sometimes when my kids
whine, I try and act just as
childish as they do. If they whine
for something, I plug my ears and in
a singsongy voice say, "I can't hear
you, I can't hear you." Usually they
say, "*Mom!* Stop it!" Keeping my
ears plugged, I'll say, "Are you
still going to speak to me like
that?" Generally, my being
childish shocks them and
they soon stop.

Some cheese with your whine?

what a hideous racket

3 years and up

Walking through the grocery store one day, one of my children (I forget which one!) started whining for cookies or candy or something. I looked at the other kids and said, "Do you hear something?" They said they didn't. I said, "It sounds like the cart wheel is squeaking." They inspected the wheels. "No," they said. The whining continued and I said again, "What is that hideous noise?" And the other three pointed to the offending sibling. I just looked at them all and said, "No, it couldn't possibly be your brother, he would never make such an awful sound." The whining stopped immediately.

Wahhh

some cheese with your whine?
smile when you say that

3 years and up

It is harder to whine when you're smiling. So tell your child that you will only listen to a request accompanied by a smile (unless, of course, he's hurt). If he wants juice, he has to smile. Want to go to the park? A nice smile, please. It will cut down on the whining—just don't forget to smile back!

some cheese with your whine?

unexpected pleasures . . .

Occasionally give your child a treat without even being asked! In her book *Your Baby and Child*, best-selling author Penelope Leach says, "If you take your child shopping and he whines for candy, you may well buy him some for the sake of peace. If you take him shopping and he doesn't whine for candy, does he get any?"

some cheese with your whine?
. . . and some
rewards

When your child starts whining less often, make sure you reward this behavior with praise. Of course, asking nicely won't guarantee she always gets what she wants. But let her know you hear her, and that you like the way she is talking to you. It's part of life to learn that not all things are possible. For instance, going back to the example when your child begs you not to go out, or to stay home with her, tell her, "Your dad and I have a special date tonight. Let's circle the day on the calendar that we are going to take you out to a movie. See, that's in two days!"

some cheese with your whine?

3 years and up

does he have a point?

If your child is asking for attention, try to give it to him.
If you've just come home from work and you want to sit
down for ten minutes before making the dinner, then make
a point of saying hello to him, compliment him on the
picture he's drawn, and tell him that you'll play a game
with him later, after you've had your dinner. Then you
might be able to get the few minutes of rest you need
without being interrupted by whining. On the other hand,
if you are on a tight schedule and are headed out the door,
don't let him disrupt your plans.

some cheese with your whine?
cut out the
house noise

3 years and up

If your child seems to whine more when your home is noisy, remember that children want to be heard. Turning off the television or the radio will eliminate background noise, so that your child will feel he can talk to you without competition.

some cheese with your whine?

civil liberty

Make sure your child understands that you won't respond to anything but civilized behavior. Explain that it's the tone of voice he's using that is the problem. Tell him you will be able to listen to anything he wants to say when he uses a nicer, less stringent voice. Simply say, "We don't talk that way." By responding firmly, you are not allowing him to succeed by his whining. Let him know that you won't give in, no matter how much of a fuss he makes. "Sorry, but I just can't hear you when you whine!" He will soon come to understand what he has to do to get you to listen.

some cheese with your whine?
whine testing

3 years and up

Help your child distinguish between whining and a pleasant voice. Model both. For one hour (or more if necessary) talk to your child only in a whine. Every time you ask your child for something, or respond to him, whine. Hopefully you'll make him laugh so hard (or annoy him so severely) that he will see the error of his ways.

Wahhh

some cheese with your whine?

surprise attacks

Surprise them with a penalty, particularly if it's something you've been through before. My six-year-old likes to sigh heavily when I ask him to do something minor, like pick up his wet bathing suit from the floor. I've warned him a thousand times just to do it happily and get on with his day, but sometimes he gives me "attitude" about stuff like that. So one day I shocked him. When I asked him to pick up a toy or two, he sighed and said, "Why do I have to do everything?" (Yeah, everything!) I said, "Oops, for talking back, you lose an hour of TV time." "But, Mom . . . " he whined. "Wanna make it two hours?" He got quiet and picked up his stuff. Now I can see him mull it over before he gives me that big sigh!

some cheese with your whine?
ban boredom

3 years and up

Younger children frequently start whining if they are having trouble mastering something. If your child gets frustrated while trying to do something, suggest another way for him to do it. And avoid challenges, like tricky puzzles or games, when your little one is tired. The opposite problem—boredom—is more likely with older children. Ask your child to help you make a list of "Fun Things to Do." Cut up the list and put it in an envelope. When he feels like there is nothing to do, he can pull out one of the ideas.

from the mouths
of babes

I have a vivid memory of something that happened when I was about five or so. In front of a group of my parents' friends, I was proving my rhyming skills, and I made quite a few people nervous when I started rhyming the word "truck." I, of course, had no idea what I said wrong, but I was sent to sit on the steps (my childhood time-out) anyway. Kids really do say the darnedest things, and it's difficult to decipher whether or not they really mean it. These tips should help you deal with cute, but foul, little mouths, whether they mean it or not.

wash your mouth out

3 years and up

Don't do it yourself. If you swear like a sailor, then you can't really expect your children not to be familiar with those words. Once it is part of the family lexicon, cursing will be a hard habit to break, especially as kids get older.

from the mouths of babes

3 years and up

the family curse

Make up acceptable family "curse" words. I have always said that if a child stubs his toe really hard and a bad word comes out, then I won't be too mad. On the other hand, there is no excuse for using a "curse" word against someone else—like you are not allowed to call your sister #@$%% stupidhead. To avoid hearing a really bad curse word come out, develop some funny words of your own: "Dagnabit," "Crud," "Sugar," are all good standbys, but try and come up with some really creative ones on your own. Yelling "Flukenfarber" at the top of your lungs when you stub your toe will almost guarantee a smile.

keep a straight face   3 years and up

Don't laugh! It's hard not to, I know. I actually heard my
little one mispronounce a common curse word once, and
it was all I could do not to burst out laughing. Because I
was sure he had heard it from me first, I couldn't really get
too mad. It is important to show disapproval and to make
it clear that such a word is not acceptable—anywhere.

This is a great time to introduce a family
"curse" word as an alternative.

from the mouths of babes
2-4 years
scream!

Screaming is loud, annoying, and painful. If you're afraid that all of the crystal in the house is about to break, make it clear that screaming is not a way to communicate with you. You can do this a couple of ways. You have to tell your child that the screaming hurts your ears and is not acceptable inside. You can also try tuning out your screaming child or walking away from her (as long as you're certain she isn't injured and is only screaming for attention).

Wahhhhhh

from the mouths of babes
give them the words

2-4 years

Teach the correct response. Sometimes children scream or yell because they don't know how to express what they want. If your child is screaming and you're pretty positive you know what he wants, tell him the words for it. Don't give him a glass of milk if he is screaming or whining and pointing to a cup. But don't be hard on him, either. Point to the milk bottle, say the word "Milk," and even if he gets a "mmm" out and nods yes, congratulate him on his effort and pour the milk. Don't give him a soliloquy to recite, but just a few simple words to show him that you know what he wants to say, and the polite way to say it. After a few times he will begin to understand that this is the proper way to request milk . . . or whatever. Use this around the house for almost everything.

didn't mean to . . .

One of my youngest's favorite things to say after he has done something wrong is, "I didn't mean to," when I know very well that he did. Children under four are not usually lying to be deceptive, but more to get out of doing

something they don't want to do. "Who pulled all of these toys out?" you might ask, only to get a "Not me." Don't focus on the lie. Instead say something like, "Well, it doesn't matter how they got here, but please help me pick them up." In the end, the child still has to do what he didn't want to do.

from the mouths of babes

entrapment

If you accuse a child of something in order to get her
to "fess up," you are only tempting her to lie. If
you saw her doing something wrong, say so.
If you're not sure, avoid attributing blame.
Don't try to get her to admit it—it might
encourage her to lie her way out of it.

Pinocchio syndrome 3 years and up

Don't lie yourself. Do your children hear you say to your husband, "Tell whoever is on the phone that I'm in the shower"? How about calling in sick to work? It might seem harmless, but in the end, you are condoning lying. I am not going to say I've never done it—and I have told my older children, for their safety, to tell people that I'm in the shower if they are home alone and they answer the phone. But it's something worth bearing in mind.

from the mouths of babes

ghosts

Are there ghosts in the house? "You didn't do it? Well, if there are only us two in the house, then we must have some messy ghosts!" Most children will pick up on how silly that idea is, and will admit to their wrongdoing—or use the "ghosts" as scapeghosts! Either way, they will understand that by blaming the ghosts, they are really taking the blame.

stay cool

The chocolate milk is all over the table, draining in streams onto the kitchen floor that you undoubtedly just mopped. When you ask your little one, "Did you spill the chocolate milk?" you will most likely get "No" for an answer. Why doesn't your child just admit it, when it's obvious she did the deed? Well . . . she doesn't want to get into trouble! Try not to overreact. Yes, lying is bad, but if you really get angry, either at the offending behavior or the lie, you'll make it difficult for your child to want to tell the truth in future. If she becomes frightened of telling you bad things that happen, then she will continue to lie. Make sure your child is comfortable talking to you about anything. I always tell my kids that most times I won't punish them for the thing they did wrong, but I will punish them for lying about it.

from the mouths of babes

3 years and up

tattling

Oh, it's annoying. "Mom, she took my . . . " There is a difference between tattling and telling—I've always said that telling is when someone, including the person you're telling on, is in danger of being hurt. Make that distinction clear to your children and remind them that, just like whining, tattling is unacceptable. Here are some ways

to deal with tattling. Say, "Hmmmm" and then turn your attention elsewhere. For a repeat offender, say, "My ears don't hear tattling," and then ignore her. Ask, "What can you do to solve the problem yourself?" or, "Is that telling or tattling?" My favorite is to ask, "Is there blood? Is anything broken?" If the answer is no, tell your child to find her own solution. Another good technique is to look directly at your child and say, "What do you want me to do about it?" If her goal is to get someone else in trouble, she will probably back down.

alternatives to
NO!

I swear some days every other word out of my mouth is "No." Or sometimes, "NO!" I've varied it a little over the years, thrown in a "Nuh-uh," and a "No way," but it's all the same. Especially when little ones are just starting to move around, there is an endless stream of "No, no, no" as they pull on cords, crash into sharp edges, pull books off the bookshelf—and no matter how much you try to childproof, they always find something to get into. Turn around—is there still a pile of dirt on the floor from when your helpful toddler emptied your house plant on the floor? Could be. Here are some ideas for variations to saying, "No."

alternatives to NO!
extra positive

Offer two yeses. I love this tool! When you tell your child to stop doing something, you simply follow it up with a few things she can do. For example, "No juice in the living room. You can drink juice in the kitchen, or have water in the living room."

alternatives to NO!
inquisition
without the pain

3-6 years

"No, Liam"; "No, Liam"; "NO, Liam." I must say that a thousand times a day, and half of the time he just keeps right on doing it. I swear, for the first two years of his life, I thought he had a hearing problem. But he always came when I offered him a cookie! It is not only frustrating to keep saying no, but quite exhausting. If your child's old enough to know what "No" means, but is ignoring you, try asking him questions. "Do you really think that's a good idea? What do you think will happen if you drop/push/kick/pull/throw that?" (Just make sure they tell you and don't show you.) Good old threatening works too—"If you do that, I'll make lima beans for dinner!" or something along those lines.

crafty
timetabling

2-4 years

Say no now, but offer to do whatever it is later. Maybe your little one just pulled out the chess set or wants to watch another *Bob the Builder* movie. Give him a specific time when you can do the activity in question, then start him on something different. The danger here, of course, is that he might ask constantly whether it's time to "watch the movie" or "play the game" yet.

alternatives to NO!
the Kissinger option

Let her negotiate a bit. This is actually quite fun. I've tried it with my three-year-old, who was just starting to use excuses and explain things. When she asks for something, ask her what the benefits are (say something like "What's good about it?"). Then ask her what's not good about the idea, or why you might not let her have it. Granted, it won't be much of a conversation at this point, but at least you'll make her work a little for the thing she wants.

"it's a tool, not a toy"

3-6 years

This is a favorite saying of my husband's. Whenever one of our children would grab something, whether it was the broom or a ball, and start "misusing" it (say, using the broom to hit the ball), my husband would ask, "Is it a tool or a toy?" The child would answer, and then my husband would give a lesson on proper use of the item in question. Children love to use tools and toys and we've let them use both, as long as they understand the difference between a kitchen spatula and a Wiffle-ball bat! This argument also works for things like fans, electronics, you name it.

alternatives to NO!

when No means No

Sometimes there is no substitute. Take the road, for example. If I had a dime for every time I heard a mother try to explain something like not going near the road to her child, well . . . you get the idea. It drives me crazy because there are just some places—and some items (like electrical outlets)— that kids just shouldn't be near. Period. And the best

way to keep them safe is just to yell "NO!" Explain later
if you have to, but scare the living daylights out of them
if they even go near the road or an electrical outlet, or
anything else that can endanger them!

alternatives to NO!

diversionary tactics

Is your child about to touch—or maybe break—something they shouldn't be near? This happens a lot at other people's houses, in particular. Tell your child, "Come here quick, I need you." And then when he runs over, give him a hug and a kiss. Tell him, "Thanks, I needed that." And then redirect him toward something else.

alternatives to NO!
substitute

This is a clever way (which I attribute to parent educator Jean Illsley Clarke, author of *Time-In: When Time-Out Doesn't Work*) to help your child learn how to do what she wants in a more acceptable fashion. Offer substitutes—you can substitute the location or the tool. For example, most children are not allowed to color on the walls. If your child wants to, you should respond like this, "You may not color on the walls. If you want to draw, you can color on paper [change of location] or draw on the blackboard with chalk [change of tool]." After you have redirected the child's activity, praise her acceptable behavior several times. This will help her to understand what is okay and what is not.

alternatives to NO!
out of sight, out of mind

3-6 years

I admit it. We have a video game system. And to be honest, there are times when I absolutely love it. I play some of the games with my kids on snowy and cold days off from school, or I let them spend an hour or two on it after a particularly bad week. But sometimes it can get to be too much. My four-year-old learned how to play with the bigger kids and all of a sudden, he couldn't get it out of his mind. And, boy, would he throw a tantrum if I told him that he

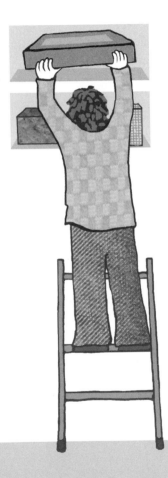

couldn't play with it. With the consent of the other children (who aren't nearly as obsessed with the games), we had our four-year-old help us pack the system away in a box, and I put it on a shelf in the closet until he got it out of his system.

alternatives to NO!

delegate decisions

3-6 years

Help your child feel more in control, so that you're not always issuing a blank refusal to his demands. Let him make simple decisions about which shirt to wear (give him just two choices: the grey or the blue shirt), or which book he wants you to read to him. This will give him practice communicating what he wants and will make him feel more empowered, and you won't have to be saying, "No," all the time.

alternatives to NO!
make it easy
on yourself

2-6 years

Get respect by being respectful. Teaching kindness and empathy for others by being kind and empathetic yourself isn't always easy. In fact, it almost never is. Still, put yourself in their shoes for a minute. Hearing "No" all of the time can turn children almost completely deaf to any word other than cookie. So try saying "No" a little less often. Make your expectations quite clear and your job a little easier: "Mama doesn't want you to stick the baby's hand in the light socket" will be a much easier directive to obey if there are covers on all of the outlets.

further reading

BRENNER, MARK L.
When "No" Gets You Nowhere: Teaching Your Toddler and Child Self-Control.
California: Prima Publishing, 1997.

CLARKE, JEAN ILLSLEY.
Time-In: When Time-Out Doesn't Work.
New York: Parenting Press, 1999.

LAFORGE, ANN E.
Tantrums: Secrets to Calming the Storm.
New York: Pocket Books, 1996.

LEACH, PENELOPE.
Your Baby and Child: From Birth to Age Five.
New York: Knopf, 1997.

LEVY, RAY, O'HANLON, BILL, AND GOODE, TYLER NORRIS.
Try and Make Me! Simple Strategies That Turn Off the Trantrums and Create Cooperation.
New York: Rodale Press, 2002.

MASON, DIANE, JENSEN, GAYLE, AND RYZEWICZ, CAROLYN.
No More Tantrums: A Parent's Guide to Taming Your Toddler and Keeping Your Cool.
New York: McGraw-Hill/ Contemporary Books, 1997.

TOBIAS, CYNTHIA ULRICH.
You Can't Make Me: But I Can Be Persuaded.
Colorado: Waterbrook Press, 1999.

notes

Acknowledgments

I would like to thank my children, my husband,
Rebecca Saraceno, and Mandy Greenfield.

index